free-motion
BLOCK DESIGNS

75+ DESIGNS

from Natalia Bonner, Geta Grama, Don Linn,
Gina Perkes, Sylvia Pippen, Kathy Sandbach,
Jessica Schick, Hari Walner, and Angela Walters!

Text, photography, and artwork copyright © 2017 by C&T Publishing, Inc.

Publisher: Amy Marson

Creative Director: Gailen Runge

Project Editor: Alice Mace Nakanishi

Compiler: Lindsay Conner

Developmental Editors: Liz Aneloski, Cynthia Bix, S. Michele Fry, Lynn Koolish, Deb Rowden, and Gailen Runge

Technical Editors: Carolyn Aune, Mary E. Flynn Helen Frost, Ann Haley, Susan Nelson, Sandy Peterson, Priscilla Read, Teresa Stroin, and Sadhana Wray

Cover/Book Designer: April Mostek

Production Coordinator: Tim Manibusan

Illustrators: Mary E. Flynn, Geta Grama, Tim Manibusan, Wendy Mathson, Kirstie L. Pettersen, Aliza Shalit, Jessica Schick, Richard Sheppard, Hari Walner

Published by C&T Publishing, Inc., P.O. Box 1456, Lafayette, CA 94549

All rights reserved. No part of this work covered by the copyright hereon may be used in any form or reproduced by any means—graphic, electronic, or mechanical, including photocopying, recording, taping, or information storage and retrieval systems—without written permission from the publisher. The copyrights on individual artworks are retained by the artists as noted in *Free-Motion Block Designs*. These designs may be used to make items for personal use only and may not be used for the purpose of personal profit. Items created to benefit nonprofit groups, or that will be publicly displayed, must be conspicuously labeled with the following credit: "Designs copyright © 2017 by C&T Publishing, Inc from the book *Free-Motion Block Designs* from C&T Publishing, Inc." Permission for all other purposes must be requested in writing from C&T Publishing, Inc.

Attention Commercial Machine Quilters: If your client brings you this book as a source for quilting designs, you may reproduce as many designs as you wish on that client's quilt *only*. If your client does not own this book, the publisher and author encourage you to sell a copy to your client. Contact C&T Publishing (800-284-1114) with your business name and resale number to purchase this book at a special resale price. For clients wishing to use designs from this book, but not willing to purchase a copy, you may reproduce no more than 10 designs *total* for commercial purposes.

Attention Teachers: C&T Publishing, Inc., encourages you to use this book as a text for teaching. Contact us at 800-284-1114 or ctpub.com for lesson plans and information about the C&T Creative Troupe.

We take great care to ensure that the information included in our products is accurate and presented in good faith, but no warranty is provided nor are results guaranteed. Having no control over the choices of materials or procedures used, neither the author nor C&T Publishing, Inc., shall have any liability to any person or entity with respect to any loss or damage caused directly or indirectly by the information contained in this book. For your convenience, we post an up-to-date listing of corrections on our website (ctpub.com). If a correction is not already noted, please contact our customer service department at ctinfo@ctpub.com or at P.O. Box 1456, Lafayette, CA 94549.

Trademark (™) and registered trademark (®) names are used throughout this book. Rather than use the symbols with every occurrence of a trademark or registered trademark name, we are using the names only in the editorial fashion and to the benefit of the owner, with no intention of infringement.

Printed in the USA

10 9 8 7 6 5 4 3 2 1

FREE-MOTION BLOCK DESIGNS

4

Design by **NATALIA BONNER**

5

FREE-MOTION BLOCK DESIGNS

Design by **NATALIA BONNER**

FREE-MOTION BLOCK DESIGNS

Design by **GETA GRAMA**

9

Design by **GETA GRAMA**

11

FREE-MOTION BLOCK DESIGNS

Design by **GETA GRAMA**

Design by GETA GRAMA

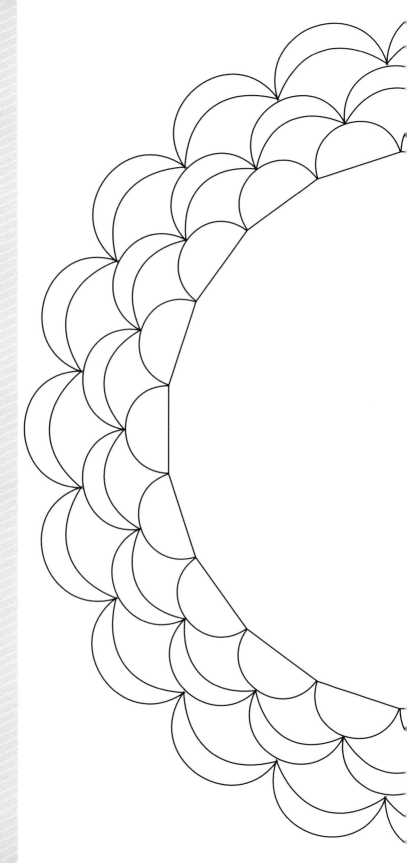

Design by **GETA GRAMA**

Design by **DON LINN**

Design by **DON LINN**

Design by **DON LINN**

29

Design by **DON LINN**

Design by DON LINN

Design by **DON LINN**

Design by **DON LINN**

Design by **DON LINN**

Design by **DON LINN**

FREE-MOTION BLOCK DESIGNS

42

Design by **DON LINN**

Design by DON LINN

Design by **DON LINN**

Design by **DON LINN**

FREE-MOTION BLOCK DESIGNS

50

Design by **DON LINN**

Design by **DON LINN**

Design by **DON LINN**

55

FREE-MOTION BLOCK DESIGNS

56

Design by **DON LINN**

Design by **DON LINN**

FREE-MOTION BLOCK DESIGNS

Design by **DON LINN**

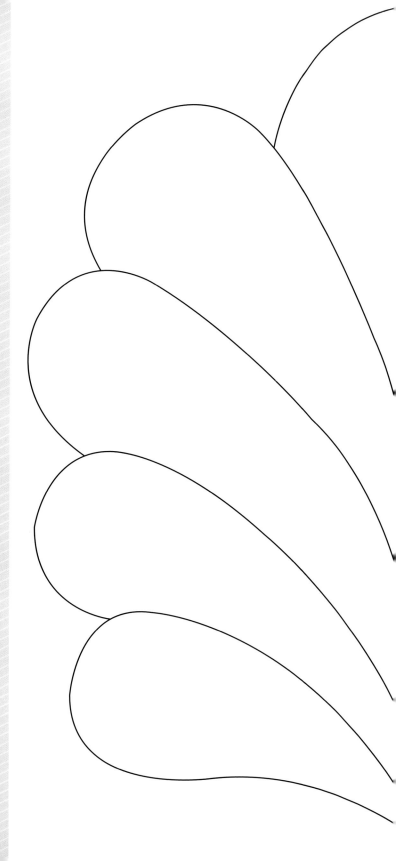

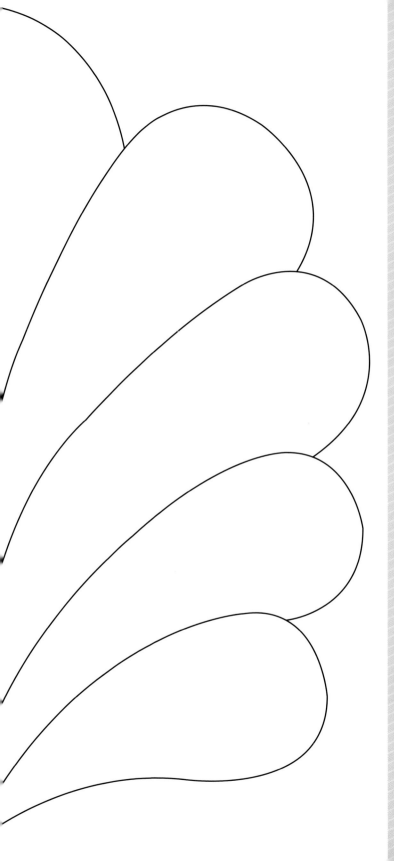

Design by DON LINN

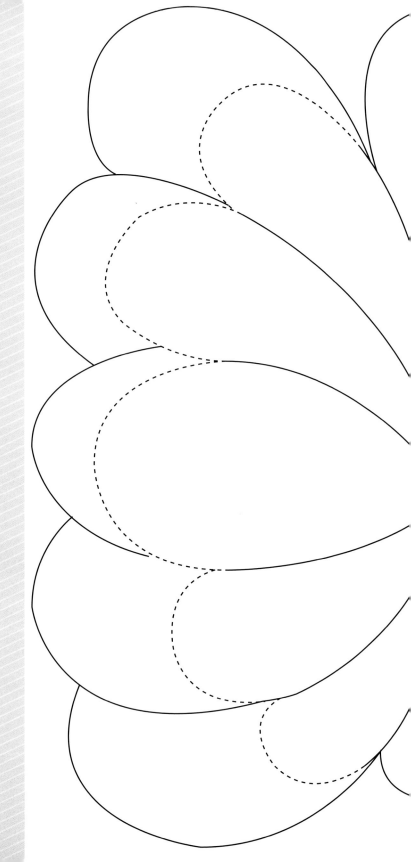

Design by **DON LINN**

FREE-MOTION BLOCK DESIGNS

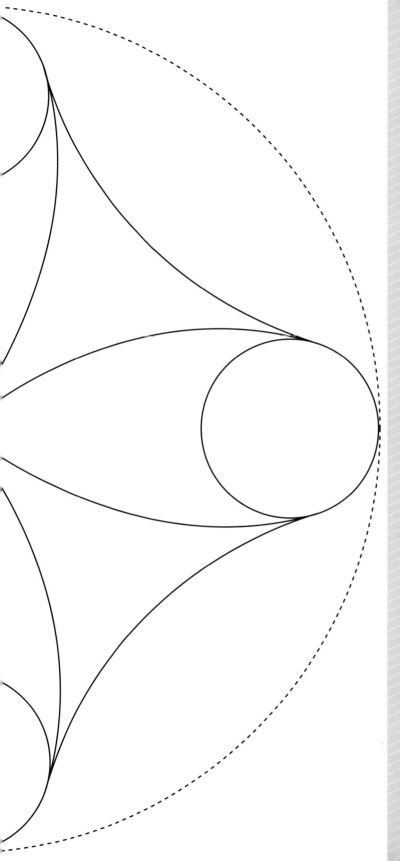

Design by **DON LINN**

Design by **DON LINN**

Design by **DON LINN**

Design by **DON LINN**

Design by **GINA PERKES**

Design by GINA PERKES

Design by **GINA PERKES**

Design by **GINA PERKES**

Design by **GINA PERKES**

Design by GINA PERKES

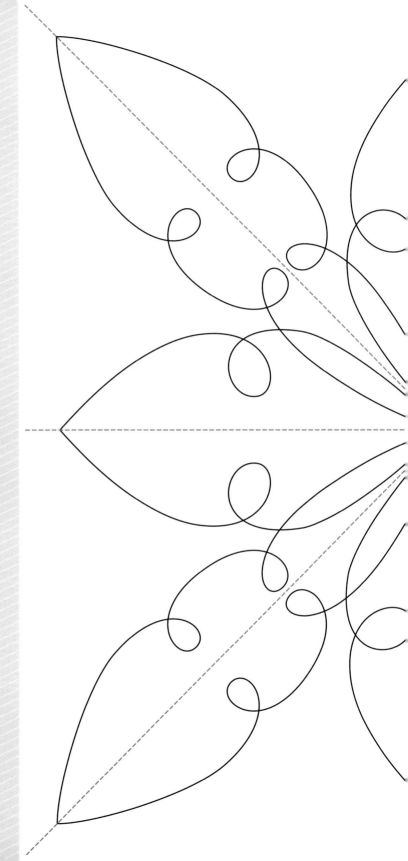

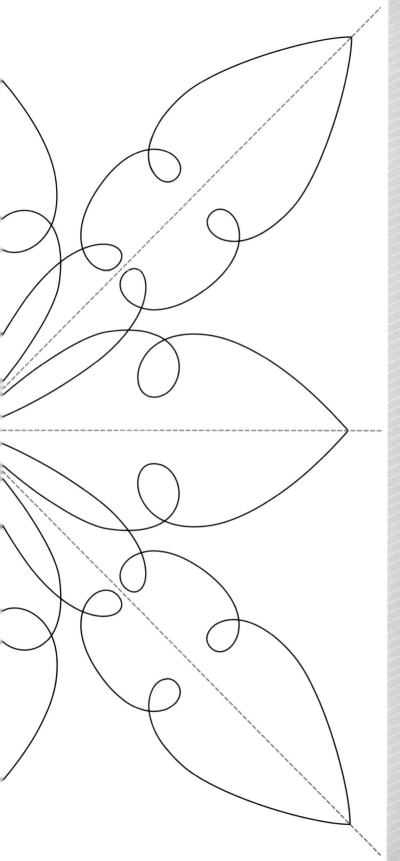

Design by **GINA PERKES**

Design by GINA PERKES

Design by **GINA PERKES**

Design by GINA PERKES

Design by **GINA PERKES**

FREE-MOTION BLOCK DESIGNS

102

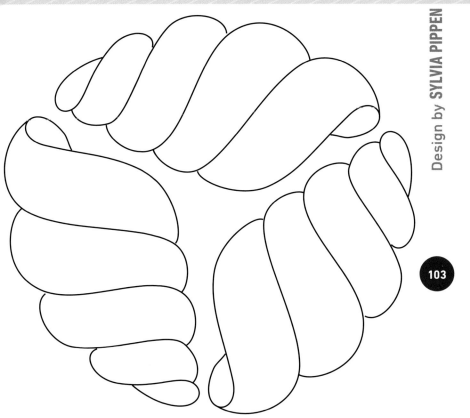

Design by **SYLVIA PIPPEN**

103

FREE-MOTION BLOCK DESIGNS

104

Design by **SYLVIA PIPPEN**

105

Design by **KATHY SANDBACH**

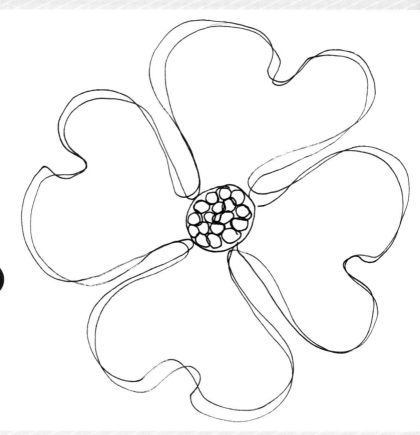

Design by **KATHY SANDBACH**

FREE-MOTION BLOCK DESIGNS

112

Design by **KATHY SANDBACH**

Design by **KATHY SANDBACH**

Design by JESSICA SCHICK

Design by JESSICA SCHICK

Design by JESSICA SCHICK

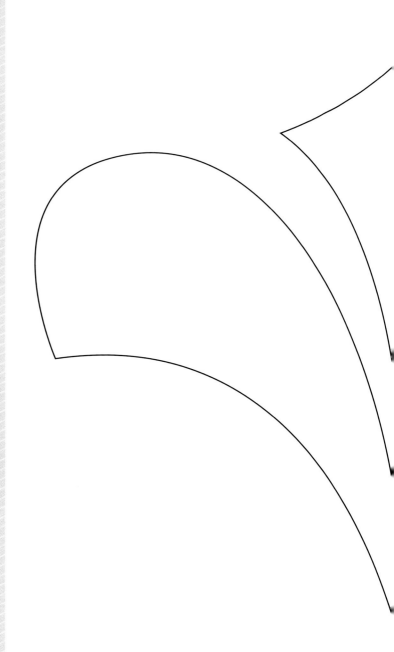

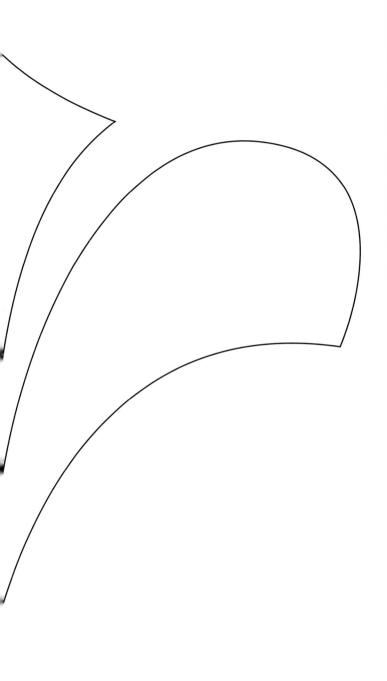

Design by **JESSICA SCHICK**

Design by **JESSICA SCHICK**

FREE-MOTION BLOCK DESIGNS

Design by **HARI WALNER**

Design by **HARI WALNER**

FREE-MOTION BLOCK DESIGNS

134

Design by **HARI WALNER**

Design by **HARI WALNER**

Design by **HARI WALNER**

Design by **HARI WALNER**

FREE-MOTION BLOCK DESIGNS

144

Design by **HARI WALNER**

FREE-MOTION BLOCK DESIGNS

146

Design by **ANGELA WALTERS**

147

FREE-MOTION BLOCK DESIGNS

148

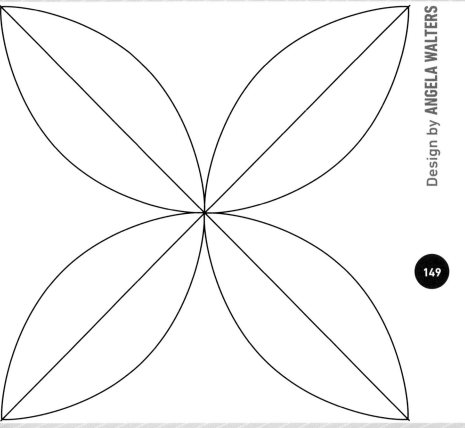

Design by **ANGELA WALTERS**

149

FREE-MOTION BLOCK DESIGNS

150

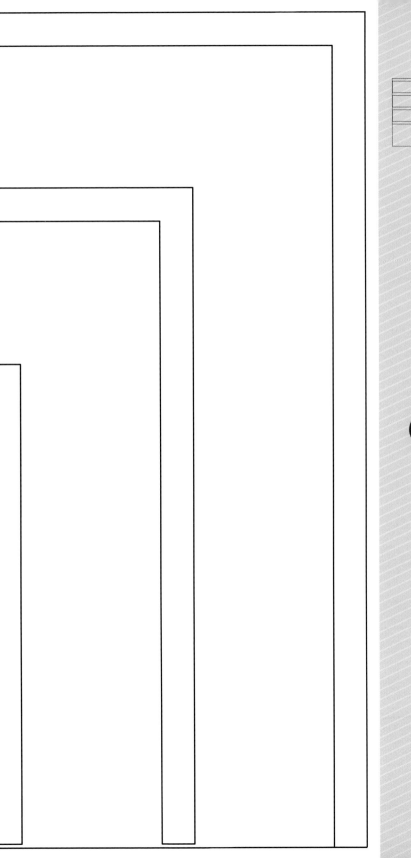

Design by **ANGELA WALTERS**

151

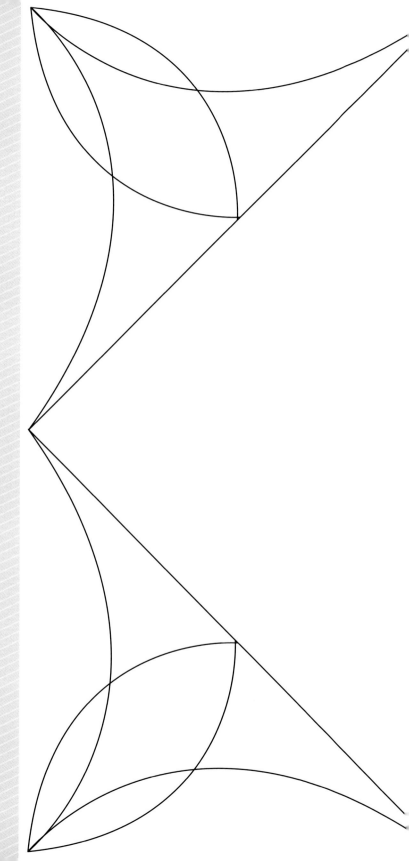

Design by **ANGELA WALTERS**

153

FREE-MOTION BLOCK DESIGNS

154

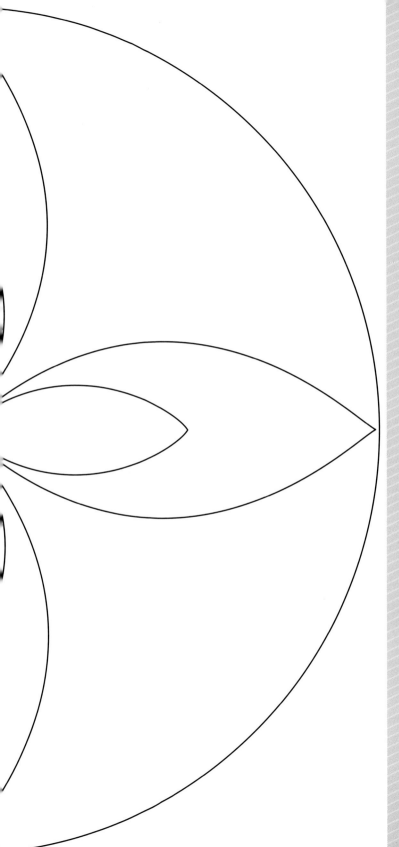

Design by **ANGELA WALTERS**

Design by **ANGELA WALTERS**

157

FREE-MOTION BLOCK DESIGNS

158

FOR MORE QUILTING DESIGNS

Check out these websites and books for more great quilting design ideas!

NATALIA BONNER   piecenquilt.com
Beginner's Guide to Free-Motion Quilting
Cabin Fever
Modern One-Block Quilts
Next Steps in Machine Quilting—Free-Motion & Walking-Foot Designs
Visual Guide to Free-Motion Quilting Feathers

GETA GRAMA   getasquiltingstudio.com
Shadow Trapunto Quilts

DON LINN
Free-Motion Machine Quilting
Design Art Deco Quilts
Sophisticated Stitches

GINA PERKES   thecopperneedle.com
Appli-quilting—Appliqué & Quilt at the Same Time!
Mastering the Art of Longarm Quilting

SYLVIA PIPPEN   sylvia-pippen.com
Paradise Stitched—Sashiko & Appliqué Quilts

KATHY SANDBACH
Show Me How to Plan My Quilting

JESSICA SCHICK   digitechpatterns.com
Quilting by Design

HARI WALNER   hariwalner.com
Hari Walner's Continuous-Line Quilting Designs

ANGELA WALTERS   quiltingismytherapy.com
Free-Motion Meandering
Free-Motion Quilting with Angela Walters
Free-Motion Quilting Workbook
Get Quilting with Angela & Cloe
In the Studio with Angela Walters
Quilting Is My Therapy—Behind the Stitches with Angela Walters
Shape by Shape, Collection 2
Shape by Shape Free-Motion Quilting with Angela Walters

For book descriptions, previews, and availability, visit C&T Publishing at ctpub.com.

Want even more creative content?

Go to ctpub.com/offer

& sign up to receive our gift to you!

Make it, snap it, share it

using
#ctpublishing